Coloring Book

I0391349

by chris

table of contents

Inspired by the ~~mind~~
heart

pt 1.

shades of black

Sleep walking

Walking on this concrete
                    floor
not knowing when your next step will be.
Knowing the foundation of what you're walking on
is more *solid* than the foundation of your future.
<u>Where</u> shall you go?
<u>What</u> shall you do?
You don't know
yet you continue in complete darkness.

Who says "the unknown is~~...~~"
if it is truly the '*unknown*'

You walk with uncertainty daily

Never knowing what's next.

Every day, we are in the

<u>unknown</u>

where am i?

Sometimes
you step foot into the pitch black
either through curriosity
or through lack of patience.
Sometimes
you begin having feelings of ~~regret~~.
Do we always lose?
Must we cope with this feeling of confusion?
Let us make <u>WAR.</u>
Helping one another through the dark tunnel of *uncertainty*.

Our biggest enemy is the <u>mind</u>.
The mind can be like a beast let out of its cage.
If you let the mind wander
it is *destructive*.

Its weapons of destruction are
"what if…?"
"but…"
and the strongest of them all

~~doubt~~

We are <u>fearful</u> by nature.
We were created with the propensity of <u>fear</u>.
We cling on to <u>fear</u> as an excuse.
We <u>fear</u> what we don't understand.
We live life limited by <u>fear</u>.
We should <u>fear</u>, ~~fear~~.

Anxiety attacks when you're vulnerable.
You tell yourself "everything is fine"
Anxiety tells you "yes, but…"
You begin to feel like your drowning
thinking "there is no escape."
"You must endure the pain" – you tell yourself.
Pain is temporary.
Stop, breathe, reflect, understand.
You are not a slave to anxiety.
YOU are in control.
Anxiety is a slave to YOU.

If I could relate my mind to a game
I'd choose jenga.
Every day, I take pieces out during my day to day activities.
When one of those pieces comes out wrong
the tower falls.
My mind is the tower.

The mind is delicate.

                              you are not alone.

                              pain is temporary.

Tic.

        Toc.

                Tic.

                        Toc.

I don't understand time.
Doesn't the same time that heal all wounds
cause those same wounds that need healing?

Tic.

        Toc.

                Tic.

                        Toc.

At times, we can sometimes isolate ourselves in our mind
believing that we are alone
in a black box with no one around to care.

Idle time is dangerous.
it allows out mind to *wander*.
Especially during a difficult season
this truly is a dishonor.

Questions ~~without~~ answers makes you wonder
if you're the only one who hurts.

Why do we choose __sorrow__ to fill our empty spaces?

People believe the world we live in only gets
darker...
Do positives outweigh
negatives?
Maybe this is the reason we fill our blanks with
sorrow...

I'm lost in plain sight
curious if anyone will ever find me.

                              <u>Hide and don't seek.</u>

Broken to the point of no return.
Yet, you make it back.

There is   h o p e.

These voices in my head
what are they saying?
Could it be lies
or maybe I'm just lost…
Or maybe the voices are telling me that I'm *lost*.

The worst feeling in the world is not feeling accepted by those who you accept the most.

Past, <u>present</u>, ~~future~~. You cant have one without the other. Although, you may wish you could forget about some memories that are held in the past, and some you wish to relive in the future.

Repetition has always been like a disease to me.
This idea that some things never change.
Change is sometimes necesarry
other times, prefered.
Repetition to some is the "easy way out."
to me, a bad habit.

Your heart starts beating fast. You begin to breath heavily. Your mind is going 100mph. Youre under attack. You begin to reflect on all the poor decisions you've ever made in your life. "Whats happening?". This is the enemy, filling you with doubt, pouring these negative thoughts into your brain. You need to remind yourself that you are good enough because you were crafted in perfection.

Trying to have the perfect life is like trying to grab a stream of water with your hands. You might think you have it, but eventually, it just drains out of your hands.

I've found trasure hidden deep within, contained inside is patience.

You sit there in silence
"theres nothing to do"
Last thing you know
youre down a day of your life you wont ever get back.

Strive for roductivity.

The sad truth of this world is sometimes the darkest seasons are the seasons under the most spotlight.

Difficult seasons causes the mind to ache.
Questions begin to stir.
You start to think isolation is the answer.

~There is more to life than the negative.~

Numbness is a addictive drug, hard to escape. You allow yourself to numb pain, but in the process, you numb other important human emotions.

———————————————————————— its not worth it.

You wonder…
"why is life so difficult at times?"
Some are more blessed than others.
You have to fight for success.
Win the battle with discipline
and be prosperous.

To the introvert,

We hate the fact that starting conversations at times are difficult.
We tend to keep to ourselves.
I've always found the introverts of this world are the most creative.
The bottled up emotions we keep inside are best expressed in art.

Being an outcast by definition just means society doesn't deserve you.

Solomon wrote it best in Ecclesiastes 1:14

"I have seen everything that is done under the sun, and behold, all is vanity and are striving after wind."

Things in this world have the tendency of eventually vanishing. We strive for material things but in reality we are just chasing the wind. The pleasure and satisfaction does not last.

Its interesting.
The most positive emotions we feel
(pleasure, satisfaction, happiness, etc.)
seem to last the shortest.
I believe through the difficult times
we learn the most.

A rainy day is good for the heart and mind.
It is like medicine for the ill.

The darkness will eventually become tired
and that is when the light shall shine its brightest.

shades of yellow

Joyful winds

Passing through the forest of contentment.
You have nothing to fear
for the joy of your heart shines light brighter than any star.

When you smile :)
you share an energy to those around you.
An energy that is inescapable.

Live every day like it is a gift.

Because it is.

You glow with excitement
to live out today.
Today holds the power to do something
you couldn't do yesterday.
A power that releases a radial enjoyment to you
and those around you.

Enjoy today, tomorrow, and yesterday.

The biggest lie lives within two words.

"I cant."

You can, you know you can, and when you do, satisfaction will fill you like a runner is filled with gratification after completing a marathon.

There is a number that always goes up
but never down.
This number holds more information than stars in the universe.
Without this number, we would never change.
This number
is age.

Light shining from the clouds.
Birds chirping with the softest of voices.
Every car is a baby blue, not making a sound.
All you can hear are the birds and the trees being blown.
No arguments, no sin, no negative energy in the wind.
~~This is the perfect life.~~

Passion is a wonderful thing
it gives our life more meaning.
Passion allows us to find pleasure in work.
Our hearts believe in doing this work
we can dent the very world we live in with our creative minds.

-

Find something youre passionate about
and witness the change it can root.
Not only in the world
but also in your very own life.

The scent of gratification is warm
its color is orange.
Gratification seeks its next deliverer
like a lion seeks its prey.
It is not out to harm as the lion is
for it seeks that the world would become as bright as the sun.

Life is an art.
Just like all art
its crafted by a creative mind.

Pursue your dreams until they come true, even if that means you have to pass through a nightmare.

There is more light in the sky at night
than in the day.
Each star produces more light
than the sun during morning.
The universe is fascinating
appealing to the eye.
The wonders of the universe intrigue me
as we will never fully understand it.

Be grateful for what you have, not for what you want.
In doing so, you will look at the world with peace and positivity.

Yesterday I was hoping for today.
Today, I was wishing for yesterday.

Wonderfully crafted by an artist who is beyond all understanding.

"Art is a form of perfection."

Struggling is a part of life.
Falling because your struggling is a choice.

Choose to stand.

Theres nothing like a good friend
when you feel like this is the end.

                                    up.

When you feel down   /\
remember to look |

Hard work and dedication is the root to all things good.

We tend to rush to conclusions.
Time is valuable
and gives value.
Allow processing
don't allow 50% to make you 15%.

There is something special about a whisper of true care.
It can transform your mood in an instant
like magic.

Moments don't last.
Cherish every second of every moment
until the moment becomes a lifetime.

The sun peaks through the clouds.
The cloud compliments the sun
and the sun is let in.

When you look into the most valuable of gems
the brightest, shiniest diamonds known to mankind.
You see a reflection
of the most valuable thing in the world.
Some may think it's the reflector
that holds the most value
but they are wrong.
It's the reflection.

Reflect on the reflection, ~~NOT~~ the reflector.

breathe in
            breathe out

You look up into the starts
all of the stars this universe has to offer.
Or at least, the only stars the universe allows you to see.
There is so much more to this world.
Seek, and you will find.
Find, and you will enjoy.
Enjoy, and you will make memories that last forever.

'Value'

FADE IN:

INT.   THE MILKY WAY GALAXY

YOU are in space, wondering why you are there.

> YOU
> Hello, space. Why am I here?

> SPACE
> You are here because you are highly favored.
> You and highly adored.
> You are special
> and no one is you.
> Only you are you.
> Prove to those around you
> you are worth the world.
> Or better yet
> worth the universe.

```
  .                 .            .       .                        .         .
      .         .          .             .           .         .                    .
    .        .                 .             .            .         .    .    (you)
  .                  .                  .      .          .
    .        .       .            . .          .                    .        .         .
(moon) .                .              .       .                    .                          .
  .                 .           .                .           .              .       .
  .      .        .           .  (earth)             .         .                    .               .
```

People will try and throw you down.
They believe by taking your ladder
they can climb up it for their own adventures.
Everyone's ladder is different.
Some, shorter than others.
Others, heavier than some.
These are simply antagonist to your story.
You must prevail, and keep on.
They will one day realize we all have different ladders of life.
Each tailored to their own adventures.
You will have the head start
while they are still learning the hard truth.

There is truth in a lie
the realization of ones character.
Stick with the true
and walk from the deceiver.
Time is like precious metals
and rust is to be avoided.

The wonders of life are amazing.
You see the trees
brown bark, green leaves.
The wind blowing on your skin
shaking the leaves on the tree, releasing a soft crackling sound.
We can sometimes get lost in the future
but lets appreciate the now.

Ugly is an opinion.
One might call something "ugly"
while another might call it "beautiful".
Art welcomes misinterpretation with open arms
allowing the viewer to define as they please.
There is beauty in anything that takes up
                                   S P A C E.

Living a life that plants a seed.
A seed that once youre gone
the next life to come will see your planted seed blossomed
into a tree.

To me, that is a life worth living.

Success to me isn't defined by money.
Success to me isn't defined by pleasure.
Success to me is defined by our happiness state of our lives.

If you are content with your work and happy with the loving people surrounding you, then to me, you are truly successful.

"One day" is an excuse we use to procrastinate the pursuit of our dreams.

Pursue your dreams today
work towards it
and never look back..

You can thank yourself later.

Even the brightest of moments can be difficult to see.
Much like how the stars are brighter than the sun.
Yet, the suns brightness is so much clearer than that of the stars.
Sometimes, we must go far and beyond to see the real light.

shades of blue

Reopening my ~~wounds~~
scars

I thought I knew you
but I only knew what you wanted me to know.

You deceived me.
You manipulated my mind.
In the end, it was a choice.
And the choice broke me.

"Who are you?"
became
"Who am I?"

To some, youre without a scratch.
To me, you are perfect.
To you, I was your puppet.

I'm trying to decide how I want to describe you, but I'm starting to think writing no description is the best description because I never really knew you at all.

I thought you would take the pain away, but you brought the pain to me.

I would have died for you, but you just pushed me off the edge.

When I needed you the most
you weren't there.
When I looked for you
you left.
You were never there.
I could tell myself you were over, and over.
But reality would eventually creep its way in
and give me a black eye.

I loved you   <3
no, I really loved you.   <3
I loved you with true love.
I poured my heart out to you
only to realized I was pouring out my heart
into a strainer.   </3

I think about you now and again.
I remember all the laughs we had
all the great conversations.
And also I remember when it all ended.

What I would have given
to make it work.
What I had given
to make it work.
Nothing was ever enough.
I would walk 500 miles for you.
You'd walk 501 miles from me.

I wonder if you still even think about me.

I thought you were my dream, but I found out you were my nightmare.

I trusted you with my emotions.
I gave you my all.
You blew it off like it was nothing.
Like my emotions were meaningless.

Love is strange. Is it the same love that brings two people together, that also separates?

You were my castle
during the storm.
You were the ear
in my difficult times.
You were my everything.

You can begin to wonder
                  most often times after a difficult storm has passed.
Will I ever find "the one"?
                                    Am I incapable of love?
Or more specifically, what one would define as "true love"?

He was your 24/7
She was your 24/7
He made you feel special
She made you feel special
He left you broken
She left you broken
He made you feel lost, and confused
She made you feel lost, and confused

They don't deserve your thoughts.
Remember that.

She searched for help, but could not find it until she realized that the only help she needed was time. Yet, time was never there for her either.

Some memories are better forgotten.

Dear you,

This change hurts but I'd be blind to no acknowledge its necesarry.

Sincerely, me.

I hope you find true happiness
like what I felt when we were together.

Relating your emotions to everything that hurts
wont help your hurt go away.
Speak your hurt
and let it leave you.

One day we'll understand
but right now I'm standing under the flames of pain.

Remember the day
it was just us under the stars.
We were dreaming about the future
talking about the next 5 years as if we were future tellers.
Now I'm alone
dreaming about the past.

She was like a shooting star.
She was a wish come true.
She was an angel come down to earth.
She was special.
She **was**.

There's no relationship without a ship to sail

far

far

       far away.

There is a red dove in my chest that wants out.
I tell it no, but it seeps it way through.
I grab it, and tell it no.
The red dove does not know what to do
for all it knows is love.
That red dove is my heart.

Your love runs like hot lava, devouring anyone it encounters. You are like a trap, waiting someone to walk through the door. Your speech is pristine, luring in those who hear.

pt. 4

shades of green

Tomorrow is going to be your best day. Why? Because today, you lived to its full potential, with or without realization. Tomorrow, youre one step closer to your dreams.

She is sad today. But tomorrow, the painful memories of yesterday will only be nothing but a blur.

Its truly a beautiful thing when you see people of completely different beliefs and paths of life come together, and live civilly with one another showing nothing but respect.

R.I.P. Nipsey Hussle.
03/31/19

The thing about tomorrow is the troubles of yesterday only have the past. Tomorrow contains the future.

Its hard avoiding the lack of gratitude we can have towards today.

Just because he has that car you've always wanted
or she has so many more friends than you
does not mean you aren't where you want to be.
It just means you can give more definition towards your dreams.

Refreshment is like a cold breeze on a busy day.
It's a feeling deeper than touch.
You feel it mentally.
Refreshment to some is a reminder of why you do what you do.
And to others, a necessity.

Fitfully a leap of faith is what you need in times of confusion. Confusion can come from a serious overload of life, and sometimes that leap of faith can charge you into uncharted waters. It might seem stressful at first, but in the long run, it's a new season of life waiting to be explored. Explore this new season, and be refreshed with a new chapter of life.

A brutal reminder for the soul
makes you think what makes you whole.

Burnout is real.

       Avoid it if possible.

              If it is inevitable, embrace it.

Rules bring limitation, and limitation brings creative barriers.

Welcome in inspiration, which leads to motivation. This steers to a constant train of production, which turns into jubilation. This is what you call creation.

Low Battery
20% battery remaining.
_____
Dismiss

Outlet. Noun.

By definition, an outlet is a means of expressing ones talents, energy, or emotions.

Listen. Learn. **Share.**

That which you don't see
is at times the thing most transparent
if you allow yourself to see that which is unseen.

There are levels to what I'd define—true—happiness and success.
You must be content with what you do.
Enjoy how you do what you do.
And find fulfillment in how you do what you do when you do it.

Even the tallest mountain can be the easiest to overcome. Its all about perspective.

What you learn throughout life isn't what's important. Its what you do with it that matters.

I go and search, and I come back with none.
I stay and wait, and I receive an abundance.

I never expected to be where I am.
But it was that leap of faith.
The step into the unknown that allowed me to be here.
I brought extra batteries for my adventure through dark room
not knowing what's next.
But here I am
using this time to reflect.

THE END.

or is it...